Dear Parent:

Congratulations! Your child is taking the first steps on an exciting journey. The destination? Independent reading!

STEP INTO READING® will help your child get there. The program offers books at five levels that accompany children from their first attempts at reading to reading success. Each step includes fun stories, fiction and nonfiction, and colorful art. There are also Step into Reading Sticker Books, Step into Reading Math Readers, and Step into Reading Phonics Readers— a complete literacy program with something to interest every child.

Learning to Read, Step by Step!

Ready to Read   Preschool–Kindergarten
• big type and easy words • rhyme and rhythm • picture clues
For children who know the alphabet and are eager to begin reading.

Reading with Help   Preschool–Grade 1
• basic vocabulary • short sentences • simple stories
For children who recognize familiar words and sound out new words with help.

Reading on Your Own   Grades 1–3
• engaging characters • easy-to-follow plots • popular topics
For children who are ready to read on their own.

Reading Paragraphs   Grades 2–3
• challenging vocabulary • short paragraphs • exciting stories
For newly independent readers who read simple sentences with confidence.

Ready for Chapters   Grades 2–4
• chapters • longer paragraphs • full-color art
For children who want to take the plunge into chapter books but still like colorful pictures.

STEP INTO READING® is designed to give every child a successful reading experience. The grade levels are only guides. Children can progress through the steps at their own speed, developing confidence in their reading, no matter what their grade.

Remember, a lifetime love of reading starts with a single step!

For John
—J.M.

To Susan Fidler
—A.L.

Text copyright © 1989 by Joyce Milton.
Illustrations copyright © 1989 by Alton Langford.
All rights reserved under International and Pan-American Copyright Conventions.
Published in the United States by Random House Children's Books, a division of
Random House, Inc., New York, and simultaneously in Canada by Random House
of Canada Limited, Toronto.

www.stepintoreading.com

Educators and librarians, for a variety of teaching tools, visit us at
www.randomhouse.com/teachers

Library of Congress Cataloging-in-Publication Data
Milton, Joyce.
Whales : the gentle giants / by Joyce Milton ; illustrated by Alton Langford.
p. cm. — (Step into reading. A step 3 book)
SUMMARY: Describes how whales live and some different types of whales.
ISBN 0-394-89809-5 (pbk.) — ISBN 0-394-99809-X (lib. bdg.)
1. Whales—Juvenile literature. [1. Whales.]
I. Langford, Alton, ill. II. Title. III. Series: Step into reading. Step 3 book.
QL737.C4 M654 2003 599.5—dc21 2002013345

Printed in the United States of America 44 43 42 41 40 39 38 37 36 35

STEP INTO READING, RANDOM HOUSE, and the Random House colophon are registered
trademarks of Random House, Inc.

STEP INTO READING® STEP 3

WHALES

The Gentle Giants

by Joyce Milton

illustrated by Alton Langford

Random House 🏠 New York

Hundreds of years ago

people believed

in sea monsters.

All kinds of sea monsters.

One story was told

about a man named Brendan.

Brendan and his friends

went to sea in a small boat.

They sailed and sailed.

Soon they were lost.

At last they saw an island.

"We are saved!"

cried Brendan.

"Let's land right away.

We will give thanks to God."

Brendan and his friends

started to pray.

Suddenly the island began to move.

It was alive!

Was it a sea monster?

No!

The men were standing

on the back of a whale!

They were so scared,

they jumped back into their boat.

And off they went

as fast as they could.

Is this a true story?

Probably not.

But some whales are

as big as small islands.

The blue whale is the biggest

of all whales.

The blue whale is also the biggest

animal in the world.

A baby blue whale

is even bigger than an elephant.

There are about
seventy-five different kinds
of whales.
The sperm whale
has a huge head.

The male narwhal has
one long, twisted tooth.
Sometimes this tooth grows
to be ten feet long!

The pygmy sperm whale is
one of the smallest whales.
It is about the size of a canoe.
That's still pretty big!

People used to think
that whales were a kind of fish.
But a whale is not a fish.
It cannot stay underwater
all the time.

A whale breathes

through a hole in its head.

This is called a blowhole.

When a whale dives,

it holds its breath.

When it comes up, it breathes out.

A big spout of spray

comes out of its blowhole.

Up it goes, high in the air.

A whale is a mammal.

Just like a dog.

Just like a cat.

Just like you!

A baby mammal grows inside

its mother's body.

This baby gray whale

has just been born.

Its mother and another whale

quickly push the baby

to the top of the water.

They are helping the little whale

take its first breath of air.

The baby whale is called a calf.

It drinks its mother's milk

just as a human baby does.

It weighs about 2,000 pounds.

But to its mother

it is still her little baby.

Usually whales are gentle.

But not always.

The mother gray whale

will fight anything

that tries to hurt her calf.

The whale calf
cannot swim very fast.
A big, hungry shark is watching.
It is waiting
for a chance to attack.

But the mother whale is
keeping watch too.

When she sees the shark,

she rushes straight at it.

Other whales come to help.

They swim between the shark

and the baby.

They are too big for the shark to attack.

The shark is not very smart.

Soon it is all mixed up.

It gives up and swims away.

The calf is safe.

All winter long

the baby gray whale swims and plays

in the warm waters

off the coast of Mexico.

But when spring comes,

the gray whales are on the move.

They will swim all the way

to cold Arctic waters.

Even the baby whale will make

the long trip.

They swim day and night.

But sometimes even a whale gets tired.

When the whales are sleepy,

they lie on top of the water

and take naps.

After their long trip

the gray whales are very hungry.

The cold water is filled

with their favorite food—

tiny sea animals,

so small you would not think

they could feed a whale.

But they do.

The whales open their mouths wide.

SLURP!

They take in lots of water.

And *lots* of tiny sea animals too.

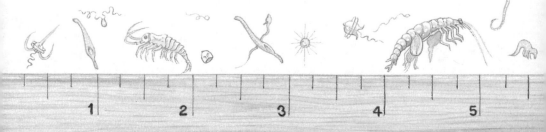

Like many whales,

the gray whale has no teeth.

Instead it has baleen.

The baleen grows in long strips.

It works like a big strainer.

When a whale spits out

a mouthful of water,

lots of the tiny sea animals

stay caught in its baleen.

They will be the whale's dinner.

People did not always know
that whales make sounds.
Sailors in submarines
used to hear strange things:
CLICKETY-CLICK! CRRRACK!

The noises sounded
like music from outer space.
The sailors were surprised to learn
that all those sounds
were made by whales.

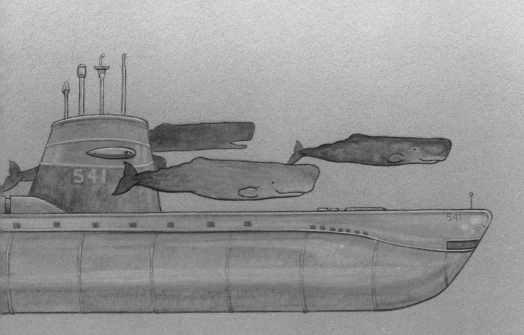

Humpback whales make
the strangest sounds of all.
They seem to be singing.
Humpbacks are funny looking.
Their heads are covered
with bumps.
But the songs they sing
are beautiful.

Scientists have even recorded
the songs of the humpbacks.
What do the songs mean?
So far scientists are not sure.

The most beautiful whale

is the black-and-white orca.

The orca does not have baleen.

It has real teeth—

big ones!

The orca hunts big fish.

It hunts seals, too.

It even hunts other whales.

Orcas are also called killer whales.

Sailors used to be

afraid of them.

Today we know that orcas
can become very tame.
Orcas are the stars
of many aquarium shows.
They like to be petted.
They love to do tricks.
Orcas are very smart.
Sometimes they even
make up tricks
and teach them to their trainers.

Orcas do not hunt people.

But for many years

people hunted whales.

Why?

Mostly they wanted

the whales' blubber.

Blubber is a kind of thick fat.

It can be made into oil.

Years ago whale oil

was burned in lamps.

That's how people lit their houses.

Ships spent many months at sea

looking for whales.

The hunters searched for whales
in the cold seas of the far north.
Sometimes the ships
got stuck in the ice.
Some never returned.

Hunting whales was dangerous work.

When they found a whale,

the hunters chased it

in small boats.

They threw long spears

called harpoons

into the whale's back.

The whale fought hard

to get away.

A frightened whale
could overturn a boat!

So many whales were killed
that few were left.
People started to worry
about saving the whales.
Laws were passed to protect whales.
Today most people who follow whales
only want to watch them.

Scientists watch whales

to learn about their lives

in the sea.

Whale watching is also fun.

Whales seem to like

watching people, too.

They will swim and play

around a boat for a long time.

If you go whale watching,

you might even see a whale

jump high in the air.

Why do whales jump?

No one knows.

Maybe they jump just because

it feels so good

to be a whale!